HABARI GANI?

(How are you?)

MAMA, BABA AND MPENDWA!

(Loved ones)

Our children receive and process messages all day, every day. They are constantly bombarded with direct and indirect negative messages about their value and worth. They also encounter negative messages about what it means to be Black or of African descent. Mamas, babas and mpendwas (loved ones) must counter the negative messages with an abundance of positive messages that uplift and empower our children…Black children!

There is great importance in what we communicate to our children about who they are, what they are capable of, where their ancestors came from, what their ancestors have contributed to the world and what they must do! If our children are to succeed, they must be inundated with positive messages about their culture, identity, education and health (exercise, eating and wellness). It is up to us—the mamas, babas and mpendwas—to carefully shape their budding sense of self.

As mamas, babas and mpendwas, we must always be aware of the messages we expose our children to. Of course this includes the things we say, but also clothing, toys, television (cartoons, reality TV shows), movies, advertisements (commercials and signs), video games, internet, social media, books, hygiene products (toothbrush, toothpaste, etc.), schools, classrooms and even people (other children and adults).

These days, most children's products are covered in cartoon characters or other popular images and messages. Though they may seem harmless, these types of products encourage our children to become consumers of items that do not reflect our culture, traditions, values or ways of life. Why do you think that is? We try to avoid buying these items and encourage you to join us in doing so.

We created **Positive Messages to Uplift and Empower Black Children** to counter the negative messages our children receive on a daily basis. We want to support mamas, babas, and mpendwas with positive messages to contemplate, recite and discuss with our children about our culture, race, community, education, people and health. We want our children to know they come from greatness and that they are great. We expect them to do great things for themselves, their families, their people, their community and their race.

WE HOPE YOU ENJOY THE ACTIVITIES!

PYRAMID BLUEPRINT

My ancestors are from Africa and made important contributions to the world and so can I.

1   www.kujichaguliapress.com

My ancestors are from Africa and made important contributions to the world and so can I.

What important contributions do you want to make in this world?

_____

_____

_____

_____

_____

_____

_____

_____

_____

_____

_____

_____

Black boys are brilliant, handsome and talented.

3

Black boys are brilliant, handsome and talented.

Describe a black boy that is brilliant, handsome and talented. If you are a black boy, describe how you are brilliant, handsome and talented.

_____

_____

_____

_____

_____

_____

_____

_____

_____

_____

_____

_____

I love my culture because it guides me and provides me with direction.

I love my culture because it guides me
and provides me with direction.

Describe how your culture guides you in a positive direction.

_____

_____

_____

_____

_____

_____

_____

_____

_____

_____

_____

_____

I love to see my brothers and sisters play African drums and dance

7

I love to see my brothers and sisters play African drums and dance.

Describe how you feel when you see people play African drums or dance. If you play African drums or dance, how does it make you feel?

_____

_____

_____

_____

_____

_____

_____

_____

_____

_____

_____

_____

I am going to use my education to uplift my family, community and race.

9

I am going to use my education to uplift my family, community and race.

Describe the ways you can use your education to uplift your family, community and race.

_____

_____

_____

_____

_____

_____

_____

_____

_____

_____

_____

_____

I love my family and I am going to make them proud of me.

11 www.kujichaguliapress.com

I love my family and I am going to make them proud of me.

Describe the ways you can make your family proud of you.

_____

_____

_____

_____

_____

_____

_____

_____

_____

_____

_____

Black girls are smart, beautiful and talented.

Black girls are smart, beautiful and talented.

Describe a black girl that is smart, beautiful and talented. If you are a black girl, describe how you are smart, beautiful and talented.

_____

_____

_____

_____

_____

_____

_____

_____

_____

_____

_____

_____

I love to help my family clean our home.

Read and discuss the following phrase with your child

I love to help my family clean our home.

Describe ways you help your family clean your home.

_____

_____

_____

_____

_____

_____

_____

_____

_____

_____

_____

_____

GEORGE
WASHINGTON
CARVER

BENJAMIN BANNEKER

PAUL WILLIAMS

SARAH BOONE

LEWIS LATIMER

I am inspired by the contributions and accomplishments of Black people.

I am inspired by the contributions and accomplishments of Black people.

What contributions and accomplishments of Black people have inspired you?

_____

_____

_____

_____

_____

_____

_____

_____

_____

_____

_____

_____

I like jogging at school because it helps me stay healthy.

19

I like jogging at school because it helps me stay healthy.

Describe the ways you and your family exercise to stay healthy. If your family does not exercise, discuss and implement a plan to incorporate it into your lifestyle.

_____

_____

_____

_____

_____

_____

_____

_____

_____

_____

_____

_____

Mansa Musa

Ramesses II

Amenhotep III

Ancient African Kings

I love learning about my ancestors who were kings in Africa.

21

I love learning about my ancestors who were kings in Africa.

Name an African king. What have you learned about him?

_____

_____

_____

_____

_____

_____

_____

_____

_____

_____

_____

_____

I love my family, community and race.

I love my family, community and race.

What do you love about your family, community and race?

_____

_____

_____

_____

_____

_____

_____

_____

_____

_____

_____

I love learning and doing math.

I love learning and doing math.

Describe what you love about mathematics. Discuss how you can use mathematics to improve the conditions of Black people. What do you know about Black peoples' contributions to mathematics? Name a Black mathematician.

_____

_____

_____

_____

_____

_____

_____

_____

_____

_____

_____

_____

If you believe in your nia (purpose), there is no end to
what you can achieve.

If you believe in your nia (purpose), there is no end to what you can achieve.

What is your nia? What does your mama, baba or mpendwa think is your nia in life?

_____

_____

_____

_____

_____

_____

_____

_____

_____

_____

_____

I am going to work with a Black organization that is committed to improving the conditions of our people.

I am going to work with a Black organization that is committed to improving the conditions of our people.

Name the Black organizations you and your family believe are improving the conditions of our people. Discuss how the organizations are doing this important work.

_____

_____

_____

_____

_____

_____

_____

_____

_____

_____

_____

_____

GIL SCOTT-HERON

HAKI R. MADHUBUTI

POETRY FOR MY PEOPLE

I love to read, write and listen to poetry.

31

I love to read, write and listen to poetry.

Recite a poem that positively uplifts Black people and discuss how it makes you feel.

_____

_____

_____

_____

_____

_____

_____

_____

_____

_____

_____

_____

_____

CANDACE QUEEN OF ETHIOPIA

MAKEDA QUEEN OF SHEBA

AMINA QUEEN OF ZARIA

I love learning about my ancestors who were queens in Africa.

I love learning about my ancestors who were queens in Africa.

Name an African queen. What have you learned about her?

_____

_____

_____

_____

_____

_____

_____

_____

_____

_____

_____

_____

I love reading books about Black history and culture.

I love reading books about Black history and culture.

Discuss a book you and your family have read about Black history and culture. What do you love about our history and culture?

_____

_____

_____

_____

_____

_____

_____

_____

_____

_____

_____

_____

I love learning about science and conducting experiments.

I love learning about science and conducting experiments.

Describe what you love about science and conducting science experiments. Discuss how you can use science to improve the conditions of Black people. Name a Black scientist and his/her contributions to the world.

_____

_____

_____

_____

_____

_____

_____

_____

_____

_____

_____

_____

_____

I am going to travel to Africa to learn more about my ancestral homeland.

I am going to travel to Africa to learn more about my ancestral homeland.

Discuss the things you like about Africa. If you and/or your mtoto (child) have traveled to Africa, describe what you learned about our ancestral homeland. Discuss future travel plans to African countries. Read books about Africa to your mtoto on a regular basis.

_____

_____

_____

_____

_____

_____

_____

_____

_____

_____

_____

We are working to achieve umoja (unity) in our family, community and race.

We are working to achieve umoja (unity) in our family, community and race.

Discuss the ways your family practices umoja (unity) to support our community and race.

_____

_____

_____

_____

_____

_____

_____

_____

_____

_____

_____

         www.kujichaguliapress.com

I am being raised in a village of mamas and babas who love me.

43

www.kujichaguliapress.com

I am being raised in a village of mamas and babas who love me.

Tell your mtoto about his/her village. Who are the mamas, babas and watoto (children) in your village? How do they show their love for your mtoto?

_____

_____

_____

_____

_____

_____

_____

_____

_____

_____

_____

I love to drink water because it is good for my body.

45

I love to drink water because it is good for my body.

Discuss the importance of clean water to your body and our people. How does water benefit your body?

_____

_____

_____

_____

_____

_____

_____

_____

_____

_____

_____

_____

In Africa, our ancestors created different types of xylophones to play uplifting music for our people.

In Africa, our ancestors created different types of xylophones to play uplifting music for our people.

What type of uplifting music do you listen to? How does the music make you feel?

_____

_____

_____

_____

_____

_____

_____

_____

_____

_____

_____

_____

I love to eat yams from Africa because they are good for me.

I love to eat yams from Africa because they are good for me.

Yams are a major crop grown in West Africa that has high nutritional value. Many West African countries have yam festivals to celebrate the harvest. Do you and your family eat yams? Have you eaten any African foods or dishes? If so, name them. If you haven't, what type of African foods or dishes would you like to try?

_____

_____

_____

_____

_____

_____

_____

_____

_____

_____

_____

_____

I am in training to be a warrior for my people in the spirit of my African ancestor Shaka Zulu.

51

I am in training to be a warrior for my people in the spirit of my African ancestor Shaka Zulu.

Discuss the contributions Shaka Zulu made to our people. What are you planning to do for our people?

_____

_____

_____

_____

_____

_____

_____

_____

_____

_____

_____

_____

ADINKRA SYMBOL GLOSSARY

We introduced Adinkra symbols into this book because they represent messages that our African ancestors created and used in Ghana and Côte d'Ivoire to express truths about living a good and decent life. Knowingly or unknowingly, our people still use these symbols all over the world. Most of the symbols we selected have multiple meanings. We want our watoto (children) to know Adinkra symbols exist and should be used as a guide for honorable living. On the cover of this book, we selected the Adinkrahene and Fawohodie Adinkra symbols because they represent our fundamental belief in the greatness of Black children and families and our desire that we should always be working towards our collective freedom and independence as a people.

Adinkra Symbol	Symbol Name	Meaning
	Adinkrahene (ah - DIN-kra - hen-knee)	greatness, authority, leadership, charisma
	Akoma (ah-ko-MAH)	Love, goodwill, patience
	Bese Saka (bes-e SAH-ka)	power, abundance, plenty, togetherness, unity
	Duafe (doo- AH-fah)	Beauty, good feminine qualities, love and care - things associated with women
	Dwennimmen (djin-KNEE-mann)	Humility, mind, body and soul strength, learning, wisdom

	Fawohodie	Freedom, emancipation, and independence
	Nea Onnim No Sua A Ohu (ne-AH on-NIM know soo-AH, OH-who)	knowledge, life-long education and continued quest for knowledge
	Nyansapo (N-yahn-SAH-poh)	Intelligence, wisdom, ingenuity, patience
	Nyame Biribi Wo Soro (n-YAH-may BEAR-ree-bee woh SOH-ROW)	hope and inspiration
	Odo Nnyew Fie Kwan (O-DO n-YE-rah fee kwahn)	power of love, faithfulness
	Sankofa (sang KO-fah)	Learning from the past to build the future

CULTURALLY UPLIFTING FAMILY WORK!

Black families should engage regularly in culturally uplifting learning activities that strengthen and help our families learn and experience new things together. We humbly present these culturally uplifting learning activities for you to engage in with your watoto (children):

1. Self-assessment (images and messages): Take a critical look at your watoto's (children's) living, playing, eating and bathing spaces. What images are on their walls, shirts, underwear, toothbrushes/toothpaste, bedding and so on? What race is the doll your mtoto plays with on a regular basis? Do these images and words positively reflect your culture, values, beliefs and lifestyle? What cartoons are your watoto watching? What lessons are they learning? Are cartoon characters on most of their belongings (clothes, toys, beddings, toothpaste, etc.)? Why do you think that is the case? Do these cartoons and characters reflect your culture, belief system, values and parenting philosophy?

2. Self-assessment (health and wellness): Take a critical look at your watoto's and family's health and wellness. Do you eat out on a regular basis? What types of food does your family eat? What types of food are in your refrigerator and cabinets? Are the food options mainly healthy or unhealthy? Do mamas, babas, mpendwas and watoto in your family engage in exercise regularly? What is your family's lifestyle teaching your watoto about the importance of health and wellness? Think critically about the messages your choices communicate about health and wellness.

3. Self-assessment (culture): What is your culture? Why is culture important? How do you show that culture is important to you, your watoto and family? What cultural images are on the walls in your house, especially your watoto's room? What cultural images are on their clothing? Do your watoto wear traditional African clothing (dashikis, lapas, headwraps, etc.)? Do you teach your watoto about their culture? What and how do you teach them about their culture? Where does your conversation about culture start? Africa, America or somewhere else in the Diaspora? Does your watoto's school teach them about their culture as a regular part of the curriculum? If so, is the information factual and up to date? What type of cultural music does your family listen to?

4. If you allow your watoto to watch cartoons, movies and online shows, provide them with culturally grounded cartoons that positively reflect your culture, traditions, values, beliefs and images:

   1. Meltrek
   2. Bino & Fino
   3. Tell Me Who I am
   4. Afroman Series
   5. Kirikou and the Sorceress
   6. Kirikou and the Wild Beast
   7. Ubongo Kids
   8. Jirimpimbira
   9. African Tales
   10. Chika: The Rites of Perdition
   11. Bouba and Zaza
   12. Black Panther
   13. Global Wonders: African American
   14. Fatherhood
   15. Abeba and Abebe
   16. Sule and the Case of the Tiny Sparks
   17. The Proud Family
   18. Tutenstein
   19. Koi and the Kola Nuts
   20. Fat Albert and the Cosby Kids
   21. Harlem Globetrotters
   22. Little Bill
   23. Golden Blaze
   24. Static Shock
   25. Brown Hornet
   26. Doc McStuffins
   27. Jackson 5
   28. Fillmore
   29. Hey Monie
   30. Waynehead
   31. C-Bear and Jamal
   32. Princess and the Frog

5. We strongly recommend being critical of the words, messages and images on your watoto's clothing to make sure they positively reflect our culture and traditions, as well as your family's values and goals for your watoto's life.

6. We strongly recommend our watoto participate in African drumming and dancing, and attend African drumming and dancing performances. We believe African drumming and dancing keep our watoto connected to our cultural roots.

7. We strongly recommend engaging and stimulating our watoto's physical, mental and psychological health by eating nutritious foods, exercising regularly and speaking words of affirmation. As a part of your healthy lifestyle, we also strongly recommend having our watoto participate and engage in self-defense training. Exercise as a family (e.g., yoga, family walks, bike riding, etc.) is also beneficial.

8. We strongly recommend providing our watoto with dolls and figurines that look like them to help them develop healthy racial, ethnic and cultural identities. We compiled the following list of dolls and figurines for consideration:

1. Makedaa Dolls
2. Natural Girls United
3. Ikuzi Dolls
4. Queen of Africa Dolls
5. Angelica Doll
6. Nandikwa Dolls
7. Unity Dolls
8. Bino & Fino (Boys and Girls)
9. Positively Perfect
10. Rooti Dolls
11. Makie Customizable Dolls

9. We strongly encourage you to read and expose your watoto to culturally grounded books that positively reflect Black watoto and families all over the Diaspora, especially in Africa.

10. Music is an important component of our culture. We must expose our children to culturally uplifting music. There are many different types of music influenced by our African roots. We recommend exposing our children to these different types, such as jazz, reggae, blues and so on. We also recommend being very critical of hip-hop, rap and R&B. Unfortunately, much of what is played on the radio, downloaded and purchased does not contain positive messages.

11. In most public and private schools throughout the country and world, Black watoto do not learn about their history, culture and traditions nor do most teachers engage them in culturally grounded and uplifting educational materials. As mamas and babas, we have to make sure we expose our watoto to educational resources that bring out the best in them. We recommend the following educational materials:

a. Counting in Kiswahili
b. Telling Time with Benjamin Banneker and Sekou
c. Kamali Academy Educational Materials
d. Let's Grow: Seed and Activity Book
e. 1, 2, 3, Let's Grow!
f. African Math: Counting 0–40
g. Maroon Life Learning Educational Materials
h. History is a Part of Me
i. The Genius Academy. org (Mathematics, Science, Social Studies and Language Arts Curriculum)
j. Imhotep's Learning Concepts Early Math Vol.1A
k. S.E.E.D.S Book Publishing Educational Materials
l. Angela Freeman Educational Materials
m. Jomo Mutegi Educational Materials
n. Black Roots Science

12. Video games, IPad/tablet games, cell phone games, and Internet-based games have taken over much of our watoto's leisure time. We strongly recommend providing them with culturally grounded and uplifting educational games and puzzles. Even when our watoto are playing, they should be learning about our rich cultural legacy. We suggest the following games for our watoto to play with one another and as a family:

a. The Africa Memory Game
   i. Afriqu'enjeux
   ii. African Flags Game
   iii. African Animals Game
   iv. Let's Go West Africa
   v. Nigeria, Ghana, & Ethiopia Trivia Game
   vi. The Africa Game of Checker Board Set

b. Black Heritage Games and Puzzles
   i. My First Matching Board Game
   ii. I Can Do Anything Board Game
   iii. The Underground Railroad Board Game
   iv. Black Heritage Trivia Board Game
   v. Elijah McCoy Puzzle
   vi. Madame C.J. Walker Puzzle
   vii. Harriet Tubman Puzzle
   viii. Buffalo Soldiers Puzzle

c. Mankala, African game
d. Brain Quest: Black History
e. Board Game: In Search of Identity: An Exciting Way to Discover Black Heritage

13. Create or find a positive affirmation that reflects our culture, values and beliefs to recite with your watoto on a daily basis. Feel free to use some of the messages in this book.

14. Create or purchase signs or posters with positive words or messages to post around your house for you and your watoto to read, recite and discuss throughout the day.

15. Create or purchase posters of Black people from all over the Diaspora who have made important contributions to the upliftment and empowerment of our people. Hang these posters in your watoto's rooms, play areas and other parts of your house.

Many of these games, puzzles, Black cartoons and dolls are hard to locate, which is even more of a reason for us to find and support them. You may have to search for them from multiple resources to locate them; don't be discouraged. We could provide websites, but the information often changes over time. It is well worth the effort to provide our watoto with games, puzzles, cartoons and dolls that represent them and our culture. As always, we recommend that you view them all first to ensure they reflect your values and beliefs.

ABOUT THE AUTHORS

Family Afrika is a Black family that lives in Baltimore, Maryland. They believe in the importance of Black families and children connecting, honoring and respecting our cultural heritage and traditions in Africa, America, the Caribbean, and the Diaspora. As a family, we work hard to learn about our cultural heritage and traditions. We practice the Nguzo Saba (The 7 Principles of Blackness) in our everyday lives and give back to our community.

The stories presented in our books are fictionalized accounts based on real events in our family and our journey to live a life that connects, honors, and respects our cultural heritage and traditions. Reading should be a regular occurrence in Black families, and it is important for Black children to see images that look like them in the books they read.

Becoming parents and watching our son, Sekou, grow up inspired these books and the stories in them. Sekou is co-author because he has contributed greatly to the books. Mama and Baba use his name as co-authors of the books to honor his contributions. We use Afrika as our last name to represent our quest to positively uplift our cultural heritage and traditions originating in Africa. Sekou has inspired us to live a life that more closely reflects our beliefs and political ideology. We strongly believe we have to create Black institutions to positively uplift Black families and children, and connect them to their cultural heritage and traditions.

Baba Sekou Afrika, Ed.D. (also known as Julius Davis) is an associate professor of mathematics education at Bowie State University. His scholarship and advocacy focuses on the intellectual and social development of Black boys and young men. He has studied and traveled to Malawi, Tanzania, and Ethiopia on the continent of Africa to learn more about our cultural heritage and traditions.

Mama Sekou Afrika (also known as Yolanda Davis) is a clinical research professional who has studied and traveled to Senegal on the continent of Africa and the Caribbean Islands to learn more about our cultural heritage and traditions.

Sekou Afrika (also known as Sekou Davis) is a student at Ujamaa Shule, the oldest independent Afrikan School in the United States. He plays the Afrikan drums with his brothers and sisters at Ujamaa. To start his formal school-based academic and social development, Sekou attended Watoto Development Center in Baltimore, MD, an Afrikan-centered institution.

Asante Sana (Thank you very much) for practicing Ujamaa (cooperative economics) by purchasing this book and supporting our Black-owned family business. A portion of the proceeds from this book will be used to support and sponsor efforts to culturally uplift Black children and families.

Your Support is Greatly Appreciated!

Baba Sekou Afrika, Mama Sekou Afrika, Sekou Afrika

KUJICHAGULIA PRESS

We define, speak and create for ourselves to celebrate our African and African American cultural heritage and uplift our people using our Kuumba (creativity).

Title: Positive Messages to Uplift and Empower Black Children
Written by: Baba Sekou Afrika, Mama Sekou Afrika, and Sekou Afrika
Illustrated By: Eloy Claudio
Edited by : Nadirah Angail
Book Design By: Eloy Claudio

Summary: This book takes parents and children on a cultural and educational journey through the use positive messages, coloring pages, writing prompts and family discussion topics.

ISBN: 978-0-9964595-3-2
For more information or to book an event,
contact Baba/Mama Sekou at books@kujichaguliapress.com.

Kujichagulia Press
P.O. Box 31766
Baltimore, MD 21207
www.kujichaguliapress.com

 KujichaguliaPress   KujichaguliaPress   @Kujichaguliaprs

#PositiveMessages
#Uplift
#Empower
#BlackChildren

Made in the USA
Middletown, DE
28 March 2022

63259116R00038